The Legacy You Leave

How to Protect and Provide for Your Family in the Modern World

Steven Andrew Jackson

Attorney & Counsellor at Law

The Legacy You Leave

Published by:
90-Minute Books
Newinformation Inc
302 Martinique Drive
Winter Haven, FL 33884
www.90minutebooks.com
Copyright © 2015, Steven Andrew Jackson, Attorney & Counsellor at Law

Published in the United States of America

140512-001-3

ISBN-13: 978-1505783353
ISBN-10: 1505783356

No parts of this publication may be reproduced without correct attribution to the author and the domain www.TheLegacyYouLeave.com.

Disclaimer: Nothing herein should be considered, or relied upon, as legal or tax advice, nor does it create an attorney-client privilege with the author. Each person's situation is different and they should hire an experienced Estate Planning attorney for their planning.

Here's What's Inside...

Why Do Estate Planning? 1

Why I Do Estate Planning.. 2

Is Government the Answer?.. 3

Who Is in Control? 5

I Can't Remember... 9

Seniors at Risk... 13

They Are Gone... 15

When the Last One Goes... 19

The Differences between Wills and Trusts... 20

Protecting the Kids.. 23

Avoid Bushwhacks... 26

Big Picture.. 29

What Is the Solution? 33

Three Questions.. 36

Here's How to Leave the Legacy You Want................... 37

About the Author... 39

Why Do Estate Planning?

Why should one do Estate Planning? You do Estate Planning because you love someone. You want part of your legacy to endure. You don't like giving away your hard-earned money to the government or to people you don't know. You want to make a difference in the life of someone else or in a cause. You really don't want to have wasted your time or your hard-earned money or your life.

Why I Do Estate Planning…

Why do I do Estate Planning? As an estate planning attorney, I have a similar vision. I want to make a difference in the lives of others. I want to help others with my skills and time. I really enjoy the relationships that I build with my clients.

You have to be able to build a relationship, get them to open up so that they will share their stories with you … their family history, the strengths and weaknesses of their loved ones and their goals and concerns. Because if they don't, you are not going to be able to do good estate planning in order to be able to help them with the plan that fits their family, their needs, their goals and their concerns.

I love the life stories from the clients. One can see patterns in the family stories. Only after understanding the client's concerns, hopes and fears, (along with knowing the strengths and weaknesses of the different family members), can I start to help them. Only after knowing these things can we begin our Unique Process of The Customized Protective Estate Planning Solution™ which we use to build a Customized Protective Estate Plan™ to meet that family's particular needs.

I have a highly protective nature which is probably why I was an offensive tackle in football and a center in basketball. I have a strong desire to help and protect others which is really why I do Estate Planning.

Is Government the Answer?

Is government the answer? We all laugh when someone says, "I'm from the government, and I'm here to help," which is not a good sign. Rarely is the government efficient or responsive in particular situations, and they are rarely the answer in estate planning.

If you don't have a valid estate plan, I mean, an estate plan that works, your assets move by the state statutes in the state that you live in, and that determines where everything you own goes by bloodline relationship.

I have seen many cases where the clients have not done estate planning or have done it improperly, and the assets go to people they have never met in their lifetime.

Anytime you are in probate court (which is where things will go if you have a Will based estate plan, or you don't have an estate plan), there is always a loss of control inside the court system. There is a large cost, it is public record, it is not efficient, and it is slow. We'll talk more about that later.

Who Is in Control?

We want to remain in control of our lives and our affairs as long as we can mentally and physically. We have achieved whatever we have achieved because of hard work and a lot of our own effort, and we don't want to give up that control. The day may come when we are unable to handle our own affairs due to a mental decline or a physical decline. Many people want their spouse to handle their affairs for them if they cannot because that is who they trust. Others choose another person or even a Trust Company.

The main thing we see on the mental disability issue is mental decline which forces us to take action on the estate plan. This is a very important part of your estate planning. If there is not mental disability planning as part of your estate plan, there is something wrong. When you choose people to be in control if you cannot be, you want to choose people who are competent and trustworthy. They are going to be the ones in charge of your affairs.

When I ask my clients about this, I will touch my chest, my heart, and say, "Who's trustworthy?", and I will touch my head and say, "Who's competent?" Those are the people you want. They may be family members. They may not be. In my situation, they are close personal friends.

When you are making decisions on who is in control of your healthcare decisions, it may be a different person that you want in control of your money. For some people, their strength is in handling medical matters but they are not good with their money so they shouldn't be in control of your money. When you are choosing someone for healthcare decisions, you want to choose someone that is going to follow your desires, not their feelings. This is a really important issue.

Many people will choose an adult child, and that adult child may have unresolved issues that will not let them carry out your desires.

When our existence is miserable, many of us want to be let go. Let us go. Let us pass on, but many family members cannot handle that emotionally due to their own issues.

Often adult children cannot accept that. They won't let mom or dad go even though that is their expressed desire because of the adult child's own emotional issues. You have to be real careful and think this through about who is emotionally strong enough and will put your desires ahead of their own emotional feelings.

Is the government in control? We rarely want the government in control in healthcare decisions.

You want to have people that you trust in control. You put the government in control if you have a Will based plan. If you have a guardianship or any incompetency proceeding, you are going to be in the courthouse. Anytime you are in the court system, there is a loss of control, plus it is public record, it is expensive, and it is slow.

You can avoid the government with the probate court loss of control with a well done, legally drafted Living Trust or Revocable Living Trust. You want to make sure that the assets are titled into the name of the Trust and that the Trust is properly administered. If it is, you can avoid the court system on mental disability and you can avoid the court system after you pass on.

As we have said, you want to make sure the Will or Trust that you create has the right person or people that you want in charge. Sometimes, people will forget and they will have chosen someone a long time ago, and now that relationship has faded. You want to have a strong relationship with the person in control. You also want to make sure you know and understand that if you have chosen individuals to be in charge, that the law firm does not place themselves in charge.

I have seen this happen a number of times where a law firm will place themselves in charge of the client's estate plan without the client even knowing it. That is something you want to make sure to avoid. "Can you trust your Trust? Can you trust your Will?" Make sure that your own attorney did not sneak a fast one by you.

I Can't Remember...

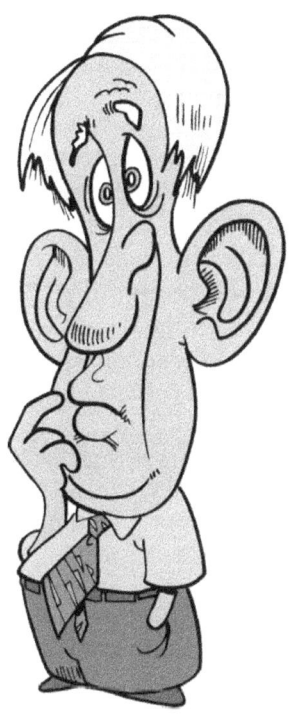

They say we are statistically six to nine times more likely to become mentally incapacitated in a given year than to die. I have worked with an administrator of one of the very large retirement communities nearby, and he said their feeling is that about one half of the residents in their retirement community at age 80 or older have some form of dementia ... some loss of mental capacity.

We think of some famous people recently who were in the news. Radio icon Casey Kasem was one of the people who declined mentally before he passed on. His adult children and his wife ended up in court over his care in both the State of California and the State of Washington because he had not done any mental disability planning.

NBA owner, Donald Sterling recently has been in court and had been involved in legal proceedings and difficulties because of his mental incapacity and mental decline. His wife was able to transact the sale of the team through their Living Trust, and the Living Trust was upheld quickly. But if they had not had that mental disability planning in the Trust in place, they would have been in court for years.

Motivational speaker, Zig Ziegler had fallen down a flight of stairs towards the end of his life and had a head injury which caused him to have dementia and affected how he was cared for.

We have all heard the stories about the billionaire, Howard Hughes, and his mental illness towards the end of his life. It is thought some of it was brought on by the numerous plane crashes that he had been involved in when he was testing new airplanes. Also, he took a lot of heavy pain medication due to the crashes which they believe had also affected his mental capacity.

Comedian Groucho Marx was involved in what many believe to be the first big televised court trial which was a trial about his mental incapacity where his adult children, who were the age of his then wife, were fighting over custody of him and how his money would be handled.

Personally, my mom and dad are good examples.

My dad died at age 84 and was as sharp as he was when he was 50 years old. My dad was very bright. My mom has had a cocktail of Alzheimer's, Parkinson's and vascular dementia for somewhere between seven and 10 years and has been steadily declining mentally. She is still the nicest person I have ever known, and she still knows me. Although now, she does not know my adult sons and she will ask me the same question about every 30 to 60 seconds. In my mom and dad's estate plan, we had mental incapacity planning which we were able to turn on for my mom as we needed it. It needs to be part of your estate plan.

In our Customized Protective Estate Plan™, we build in a mechanism for mental disability. We create a panel of your attending physician and who you choose as the loved ones to decide if we need to flip on the switch to turn on the mental incapacity part of the Trust. We are very specific as to who gets taken care of out of your money. Make sure that the money is used for you and not others if you don't want it to be.

Be real specific as to how you want to be cared for. Do you want to stay at home as long as medically and financially feasible? If you have to be in a care facility, is there a particular town you want to live in? Do you want to live in Western North Carolina, or do you want to live near a particular adult child or loved one or best friend? Who do you want to choose the care facility, if one is needed?

You can design these in your Living Trust. The goal in all of these situations on mental disability is staying out of the court system. If you do an adult incompetency or guardianship proceeding in North

Carolina, you are filing a lawsuit, notifying all the relatives and any interested parties that there will be a trial. You list all of the assets of the person, so literally, the person that gets the paperwork as part of the lawsuit can see how much money they have.

Then, there is a trial and you go to court, and the parties go to court. It can be a jury trial. It can go on for a lengthy period of time, and the first question is, "Are they mentally competent?", and the second one is, "Who gets control of the individual?" correspondingly, "Who gets control of his or her money?"

That is the downside of going to the court system. Again, any time you are in a court system, there is a huge loss of control because all the judge knows is who is right in front of him for a very short period of time. They don't know the family history. They don't know what people are like. Bad people can present well for short periods of time.

Seniors at Risk...

When we think of seniors, a lot of seniors will be taken advantage of. Part of the Donald Sterling story (who was the wealthy owner, along with his wife, of the Los Angeles Clippers NBA basketball team), was that in about a year, he had given out $1.5 million in gifts to a girlfriend. This was while he was mentally incapacitated. He was being taken advantage of and his wife filed a lawsuit to try and set those gifts aside.

You want to watch mom and dad or your loved one to see if they are mentally declining because there are predators who will take advantage of them. There was a repairman in a nearby town who called himself 'The Widow's Helper', and he would do light repair work and charge seniors about five times what it was worth. I ran across him a couple of times regarding senior clients. You want to watch, if you are the one helping take care of your loved ones, to see if they are declining mentally. Make sure that you can protect them legally.

They Are Gone...

If someone has died, what do we do next? There is a comedy play called *Daddy Died, Who Has the Will?*, which is a chaotic comedy of everyone scrambling around, trying to find the Will and find out what daddy owned. You want to avoid that.

You can have a well done estate plan prepared by a qualified estate planning attorney. The attorney can be working (if you want them to) with your adult children (not necessarily knowing what your assets are) but they could know what the estate plan is. That way they know what their roles are when they come into play either as the healthcare agent or the successor trustee. Your estate planning attorney should work with your other trusted advisers such as your accountant or your financial adviser and your insurance professional.

You want to have the estate plan set up in advance. You want to make sure that the estate plan is current with the law, current with your relationships and current with what your desires are. You want to make sure that all of your assets are titled into the name of your trust so that they can skip probate court. You want to make sure that the successor trustees have met with the estate planning lawyer so that they understand their role.

We have what we call 'Family Meetings', and we will try to meet with the adult children (or others) who help come in and take over the estate plan if someone has declined. That way, they know their roles, the adult helper knows their role when they come in to help mom and dad, and it is less chaotic. If you try to teach someone while the person is declining in health, has become mentally incapacitated or has passed on, the emotions are running so high, it is hard for the survivor spouse or the helper to effectively operate within their roles.

When we do the estate plan and put it together in our estate planning portfolio, not only do we put together the estate plan and all the supporting pieces such as all the healthcare powers and everything else, but we also try and put in what assets the client owns. That way, when the adult child comes into play, not only do they know what the parent's desire is, they know where the assets are. *'What investment accounts? What bank? Where is the deed to the house? Where is the title to the automobile? Is there land in another state?'* That is much easier than trying to look through the sock drawers or through the old bank statements and trying to figure out what mom and dad owned after they are incapacitated or deceased.

The same thing is true with the healthcare powers. These are really going to come into play as seniors get older. If you get sick or have a stroke or have a heart attack or whatever it is, your healthcare agent needs to be in a position to help you right away.

Often, after someone passes on, his or her surviving spouse has a very difficult time trying to come in and take action. It is almost like somebody has whacked them in the head with a baseball bat, because they are distraught, their partner of however many years or decades has gone, and they are so overwhelmed that it is hard to move forward and take action that needs to be taken. Many times, the adult children will need to step up to help. It is better if everyone is prepared ahead of time while everyone is calm and coherent.

In our formal update program, The Life Plan System™, we present our Nuts and Bolts™ workshops. These are big versions of family meetings where we talk about how the estate plans work and the helpers' roles. We will do them at Thanksgiving and at Christmas because that is when the adult children come home. We do them in a workshop style. *'What do we do if you are the healthcare agent when you come into play? What happens if you are the successor trustee? What do you do if dad passes? What do you do if mom passes? What do you do when somebody gets sick? What if there's mental disability?'*

We never talk about the client's assets or how a specific plan works, but we give an overall view of what the roles would be in the structure of how the estate plans work. This is a much better way for the adult children to try and understand, and it also gives us a good chance to talk about the elephant in the room which is *'mom and dad are going to declinc to the point where they are not here.'* Legal action has to be taken to administer the estate plan, so it is better if your helpers are ready to start moving forward as needed.

People will talk about powers of attorney, but they can be difficult to use. Often, financial institutions won't follow them or use them if they are more than five or 10 years old. Also, they can be too broad. There is no reporting requirement and there are no instructions on how to do anything so they really can be used to take advantage of people. Our goal is keeping you in control as long as we can both medically and financially, and by having the right people in place that you trust to take care of you if you decline mentally and when you pass on. They have to be the right people in control. We want to stay out of the courthouse.

We try and push for the clients to have funeral instructions in place. *Do they want to be cremated? Is there a pre-need funeral arrangement already made?* A lot of fights in the families are over this. *Did somebody want to be buried? Or cremated? Or caskets used? Or scattering of the ashes?* Also, there are a lot of fights over where the assets go after somebody passes on. *Do they go to the surviving spouse alone? Do they go to other loved ones?*

Blended families are always a hotspot and potential for conflict because you will have a spouse that mom or dad may have enjoyed and gotten along with well. Then you have the adult children who have known and loved mom and dad much longer than the person that they married later. So anytime you have the blended family, there is a lot of potential conflict and it is always a balancing act with the estate planning lawyer and the clients. The estate planning lawyer should have a number of conversations with the clients about potential conflicts and avoiding them because you don't want your children to have conflict with your surviving spouse. You want everybody to try and get along, in the same way you want the adult kids to not have conflict with each other after you are gone.

When the Last One Goes...

You can avoid probate court if your estate plan is well designed and current. When you pass on, when your spouse passes on or your loved one, parent, et cetera, pass on that is when we look at the questions of: *'Where is the estate plan? Is it a valid legal enforceable estate plan? Are we going into probate court? Where are the deeds? Where are the bank statements? Where are the investment accounts? Where are the titles to the vehicles? Are they in multiple banks? Are we looking at multiple pieces of real estate? Are there retirement plans? Is there life insurance?*

The more we prepare ahead of time, the better. We work with our clients to try and put their records of assets with their estate planning portfolio so that everything is in one place. If we don't do that, the adult children are not going to know what mom and dad own or the instructions of the estate plan. We look at *'Who is in what role?'* Again, we can have different people in the healthcare role versus the trustee handling the assets role.

One of the questions is always, *'Can we avoid the court system?'* The court system, or probate court, is slow, expensive, costly, and public, so we are always looking to avoid it at all times. There are different ways that people leave their estate. Some people say, "After I'm gone and my spouse is gone, then divide the assets and give them to our children, adult children or whoever the loved ones or friends are, and just move the money out." Others say, "Protect the assets and move them out over time to my loved ones so that they cannot squander the inheritance."

The Differences between Wills and Trusts...

A Will is only effective when you pass on. It forces you into probate court. It is public record showing who inherits, how they inherit, and how much. The Administrative Office of the Courts tell us that the average administrative time is between 18 and 24 months from the time the Will goes to probate court until the time you can pay the money out.

The Court costs are up to $6,000.00 per person or $12,000.00 per couple and there have been discussions that costs may increase to $9,000.00 per person soon. The average administrative fees are 5-7% and that is what the attorney's fees normally are. So 7% of $1,000.000.00 would be $70,000.00 in extra fees. There is a probate per state where you own land. If there is a Will Caveat, it is a jury trial and the attorney fees for all attorneys are paid by the estate assets.

If you have a Living Trust based plan and all of your assets are titled in the Trust, and the Trust is properly written and administered, it has the many advantages of avoiding probate court. You can do mental disability planning inside of a Trust, whereby you do not go through court. The Trust's terms are private as to who receives the inheritance, how they receive it, and how much. It can take weeks to months to administer the Trust as opposed to years to probate the Will. There are no court costs. The administrative fees are 1-2% as opposed to 5-7%. There is no probate court for out-of-state real estate. If there is a lawsuit, it is ruled on by a judge and each of the parties pay their own attorney fees as opposed to the attorneys being paid out of your probate assets in a Will Caveat lawsuit. It is much harder to break a Trust.

Bare Bones Trusts – versus – Protective Trust Planning

A "<u>Bare Bones Trust</u>" is a short document.

This "Bare Bones Trust" may not be effective in another State.

There is little to no Protective Planning for the surviving spouse or children and no detailed Mental Disability Planning in a Bare Bones Trust. Bare Bones Trusts are often just an 8-20 page document. They are often created by what are commonly referred to as "Trust Mill Lawyers". They just "Search and Replace" or plug in the names on a document and crank out the documents. Some Law Firms provide them. Sometimes Banks provide them (which is the practice of law without a law license, which is a crime in North Carolina). They are found On-line or as a Do It Yourself document. Also Financial Sales Representatives may sometimes provide them with a statement of "buy an annuity from me and I will get you a Trust".

A "<u>Customized Protective Estate Plan™</u>" can skip Probate Court as to the Assets titled in that Trust. Also, it can provide some protection for you and your loved ones in the event of remarriage, lawsuit or Mental Disability. The attorney has to spend time with you asking questions about you and your loved ones. They must know what you value and your goals and concerns. Otherwise they cannot prepare a "Customized Protective Estate Plan™" that meets you and your loved ones individual needs.

This plan we create should work in other states.

Such an Estate Plan can do Mental Disability Planning. It can provide a Panel who will determine if you are mentally able to handle your medical and financial affairs. You can state your preferences for how you want to be cared for if mentally disabled. Do you want to stay home or do you want to choose a particular care facility? Do you want to name a person to choose such a care facility?

The "Customized Protective Estate Plan™" can provide some protection for the Surviving Spouse. Such protection can include Remarriage Protection for the surviving spouse to limit their being taken advantage of in the event of a remarriage. It can also provide some Car Wreck Lawsuit protection for the surviving spouse.

Such detailed planning can provide some protection for your Adult Children in the event of Divorce, Squander or a Car Wreck Lawsuit. Further, it can provide additional planning for Special Needs, Addiction and other issues. Often it will have Tax Planning designed within it.

A "Customized Protective Estate Plan™" must be done with an Experienced and well qualified Estate Planning Attorney. An Attorney who spends the time with you to find out what your particular concerns are and the strengths and weaknesses of your loved ones. The experienced and listening Estate Planning Attorney creates the additional needed protection for you and your loved ones that a "Bare Bones Trust" does not.

Protecting the Kids...

A lot of estate planning attorneys think that assets should be kept in trust for the adult children for their lifetime and not paid out right upon the death of the parent. You can do that and still give the adult children control of their share. A risk to the adult children that is out of their zone of control is divorce. When the inheritance comes in, if your child's spouse goes out the door and they have put that money in joint names, half of it just left your family. They say the divorce rate is over 50%.

Creditor protection - you could be in a car wreck and you could be sued. We all cross the double yellow line, most times there is not an accident. But if there is one and it is your fault, whatever you own can be lost. If it is in a protective trust under the inherited trust of mom and dad, it might be protected and not be available to creditors and lawsuit.

You can keep the adult children from squandering the inheritance. You can pay the adult's creditors directly or pay out the money over time like an annuity to the child.

The parent can incentivize good citizenship or behavior. There was a front page article a number of years ago in the *Wall Street Journal* about Tom Glavine who was a very successful professional baseball pitcher with the Atlanta Braves. He talked about incentivizing his children because he didn't want them to just sit around and be spoiled brats from an inheritance. So he set it up to incentivize them in certain ways. "If you will work and make money, you will get extra money. If you will do charitable work, we will give you extra money and money to the charity."

If you want the adult daughter or son's spouse to stay home with the kids, we will replace that spouse's income that they would have earned in the work force. Most times the family will want the inheritance to stay in the bloodline. Do you want it to go to your kids? Do you want it to go to your grandkids? Do you want to provide education for your grandkids or multiple generations downstream?

If you have certain charities you like, you can help by providing money to a charity that could help people that couldn't otherwise be helped. You may want to help nature conservancy or the Sierra Club, or help the homeless, or provide clean water in foreign countries or whatever it is.

There may be other people that are not your children but they are like your children. They grew up in your home or they have been loyal and faithful to you, and you might want to reward them financially.

Avoid Bushwhacks...

Avoiding bushwhacks includes avoiding probate court. I know I am repeating myself here, but this is a common area of misconception. The downsides of probate court are numerous. The attorney fees, which they often refer to as 'administrative expenses', can be 5-7% of the value of your probate estate. For example, if you have One Million Dollars of assets moving through the Probate Court, the attorney could get a $70,000 attorney fee. There are also court costs in North Carolina. Court costs are a version of a tax on the assets that are moving through your probate estate. They can be a cost of up to $6,000 per person or $12,000 for a couple. There has been talk of moving that number up to $9,000 per person.

Time delays – we have been told by the Administrative Office of the Courts that the time delays on the average probates are somewhere between 18 months and possibly 24 months. This means that from the time you put the Will into the courthouse until the time the courthouse says, "You can now pay out the money," can be a year and a half to two years.

Here in Asheville, North Carolina, there is one disputed probate that has been in litigation for 16 years and it is not over yet. Everything is public record when you are in probate court. *Who gets the money? How do they get the money? How much?* They are all public record.

There is a huge loss of control when you are in the court system because the court is in control, not you, not your family. Ever since I have been a lawyer, I have always felt that there were, what I would call, 'scavengers' in the courthouse hanging around the court system, and they are looking to pick up assets cheap or at a reduced cost out of a probate court or out of a divorce.

Creditors and predators - some of them are the vultures of the courthouse or they are doing it electronically now because it may be public record. There could be other ones too.

My mom used to talk about when there was a widower at church and the widows would start bringing pies and cakes to the widower, but yet, they didn't bring pies and cakes to the widows. My mom did not like that. Again if there is a late remarriage or blended family, we have to balance the estate plan. We want to pay attention to that balancing act when you do the blended family estate plan.

You should have remarriage protection in your estate plan if one of you passes on and the surviving spouse remarries. You will want to have some protection built in the plan that says '*The new person has to sign a prenuptial agreement*'. Something along those lines with the theory being, '*Let's keep the money in our family as opposed to going to somebody else's family members.*' We can design that in a well-designed estate plan.

You can build in lawsuit protections from a car accident lawsuit. Inherited IRAs may or may not be creditor protected. In some states, they are, but in other states, they are not protected from a creditor in a lawsuit. People move from one state to the other and the laws change.

Another thing I have learned as a lawyer is that just because something is a law right now doesn't mean it will be the law in five or 10 years. You will have a different legislature and, a different political party may be in control with a different agenda.

Also, some adult children are their own worst enemy. They may squander the money, squander any inheritance and blow it all in a year or two years. You can set it up so that the money comes out over time in slow monthly payments so that they have access to the money but they can't blow it all up at one time.

Is there a hidden trustee in the Trust or person who runs the Will? Can you trust your Trust? One of the things that has been unusual that I have seen recently is lawyers that will place themselves inside your estate plan as the successor trustee after you are gone. You don't realize that it happened. They don't tell you. You believe the one you chose is going to be your successor trustee.

Yet the law firm or lawyer has put themselves in the fine print, name themselves as a 'Trust Adviser' and then later refer to the trust adviser as the successor trustee so you don't see their name listed in the trustee section. If you don't know what is happening, after you are deceased, it is too late to fix it and too late to modify it

You don't want to pay unnecessary estate taxes, capital gains taxes or income taxes. Those are pieces you want to watch out for when you are designing the estate plan.

Big Picture...

Again, if you do not have a valid estate plan, the state has one for you. It will move the assets by bloodline, and it may go to people you don't know or have never met.

There is a strong reason greed is one of the seven deadly sins. Greed brings out the worst in people. That includes trying to get your trust assets.

If your estate plan is poorly designed or poorly implemented, you may be setting up a fight within your family. Many family members never speak to each other again after an estate is settled. Dr. Phil even has a section on that on his website and has done a number of TV episodes about that.

There are creditors and predators that you have to watch out for while a senior is mentally incapacitated.

You don't want to set up a fight between the adult children or between the second spouse and the adult children by doing poor estate planning. One of the worst things you can say is, "I will let the kids fight it out" or "I will let the kids figure it out." Be specific about what happens so that the kids aren't in a situation where they are in a dispute where you have created conflict.

A retired Florida estate planning attorney who moved up here to the mountains asked me to do an estate plan for him and we became pretty good friends. I asked him how often he felt there was acrimony or conflict between family members in settling an estate, not necessarily a lawsuit, just ill will between each other. He said one out of three times in an estate settlement. To me, it seems like maybe one out of five.

Business owners who have spent a large part of their lifetime building a business from scratch are often the ones that don't do estate planning or don't do good estate planning. If they don't, they have lowered the value of their lifetime work in the business immediately when they pass on. You need to do estate planning ahead of time. You need to do the estate planning specifically for the business ahead of time.

It is always funny how some people think they won't ever die, and I have literally heard people say, "If I die," as if they won't. I wonder if they know something the rest of us don't. As my dad used to say, "None of us are getting out of here alive anyway." We do need to plan for our estate.

One of the things that is interesting is people have the tendency to do estate planning when their children are young because their concern is, *'If we are both killed in a common accident, what happens with our children? Who takes care of them? Where does the money go? How does that work?'* Then they again look at their Estate Plan, when they get more in their 40s, 50s and up where they are seeing, "I'm getting older. I need to prepare for this." Sometimes, when the clients get up in their 80s, they won't do estate planning. They are afraid that if they do that they jinx themselves. However, if you don't do an estate plan, you are setting up chaos in the family.

I have seen a play in life which is how I would

describe it, and it is when the lion or lioness, the head of the family, the matriarch, the patriarch in the family, goes down either by mental disability or they passed on. I see the adult kids come in to the play and start taking action. Often, I will see three characters. One of the adult children will play the role of Switzerland, and they'll say, "Let me stand over here on the sidelines. Mail me a check when it is over. I don't want to get involved."

Often, there is what I call 'The Dutiful Child'. The dutiful child will step up and say, "What did mom and dad want? What work needs to be done? What's the right thing to do?" Then, you will often have a third character who says, "How can I take advantage of the situation?", who will try and move mom or dad's money to themselves during a mental disability or death outside of what mom and dad wanted in the estate plan.

If you ask a senior who is winding down towards the end of their life, their biggest regret is most often something they didn't do, an experience they didn't do. Is there something you are thinking about saying to someone or haven't done? What is holding you back? It can be something as small as an encouraging visit, phone call, note or email.

I like handwritten notes, something on paper that you hand write out and mail. It is something they can stick in a drawer and go back and look at later. Something you can do for someone else is a thoughtful estate plan that carries out your legacy and helps others without sending unnecessary money to the government. You can do the estate plan so that it avoids conflict between your loved ones.

I have a book that I have read that was sent to me when I graduated college, and it was by Charlie "Tremendous" Jones, a little thin book. In essence it said: there are really three big questions in your life that determine everything. What are you going to do with God? Who do you marry? What is your career? Everything spins off of that.

An old farmer friend told a friend of mine when my friend was getting married, "If you marry the right person, there is nothing better you can do to improve your life. If you marry the wrong one, you might as well have a broken back in hell." It seems like a funny story, but in reality, it is true.

Some Native American Indians say, "As long as someone is telling your story, you are still around." What story will they tell about you? I knew an older lawyer here in town who had turned his tumultuous life around in a good way after struggling for years with alcoholism. He told me that his goal was to make one person smile every day. He told me this one when he was in his 70s and practicing law. I only knew him as a sober person, and he regularly had a huge smile and shared it constantly.

I regularly ask my young adult sons, "Are you part of the problem or part of the solution?" I tell them, "You can only really have one of two attitudes. You can either think the world revolves around you and your desires and others exist to serve you in which case you will be miserable as it does not, or you can choose to be thankful in all circumstances and look at challenges as lessons to learn from. You are more likely to be content and thankful with that mind set and have a happy life."

What Is the Solution?

What is the solution? In estate planning, it is easy for things to go poorly if the estate planning is not done well. In our unique process, The Customized Protective Estate Planning Solution™, we have a regular process that we go through which gives us a much better chance of doing a good estate plan for the client that will help protect them and their loved ones and their legacy.

In the first step, we gather and review information from their existing estate plan and gather information regarding their family and how assets are owned so that I am well prepared for the first meeting. I also have a good idea of what their goals and concerns are. In our first meeting, we work together to identify what the strengths and weaknesses of their loved ones are and what are their assets and how they are owned. We work to find their goals and concerns.

From my more than 30 plus years of legal expertise plus my own life experiences, I help the client understand how the estate planning works, how we can protect and provide for them, and the clients can teach me about their family's strengths and weaknesses. You just keep asking questions. If you don't know the client's loved one's strengths and weaknesses or the client's concerns or goals, you cannot do good estate planning in my opinion.

After we have a good understanding of the clients' goals, the strengths and weaknesses of their loved ones, and their assets, we can begin designing a Customized Protective Estate Plan™. We can plan for Mental Disability and plan for what happens after the first one passes, and then what to do if there is a remarriage of the surviving spouse, and how to protect their loved ones in the event of a lawsuit or divorce.

There may be special needs planning for challenged or handicapped individuals, or there may be drug, alcohol or gambling addictions in the family. There may be a concern that the adult children are going to squander the inheritance. We may want to protect and provide for education for grandchildren or other generations.

We plan to avoid taxes and probate cost. Probate costs can be very expensive as we have discussed, and also if we hit estate taxes, they can be very expensive. When we meet to review and sign the estate plan, we go through it page by page to make sure the client knows and understands the plan. What I hear from others is, the lawyer just says, "Here's your plan. Sign here, here and here," and the client never goes through the plan so they don't know if it actually does what they think it does.

We work with the client's trusted advisers who may be their financial advisers, their accountants, and their insurance professionals so that we make sure that the plan will work from a financial standpoint, an insurance standpoint and tax efficiency standpoint. When the plan is in effect after it has been reviewed and signed, assets have to be retitled into the trust so that the protection and

control of the trust is in place.

That can include retitling the land, retitling the investment and bank accounts and other assets that have a title. They all go into the name of the Trust.

We have a formal update program that is The Life Plan System™ where we work to keep the plans up-to-date with the law, and we have our classes for the client's loved ones that we have discussed, the Nuts and Bolts™ Workshops. We do these at the holidays. We also do family meetings and other work that we do to keep the estate plan current.

Three Questions...

There are really three questions to ask yourself as you think about estate planning. Those questions are as follows:

Number one, '*What are the most important things in your life?*

Number two, '*What are the most important relationships in your life?*

Number three, '*What legacy will you leave?*

You can leave a lasting, very impactful legacy of good if you do thoughtful estate planning. You will need an experienced estate planning attorney who will work to understand your goals, concerns, and the strengths and weaknesses of your loved ones. That estate attorney must put protecting you and your loved ones as the top priority.

Here's How to Leave the Legacy You Want...

You already know you want to protect yourself and your loved ones when you become mentally disabled or pass on. The confusing part is not knowing how to keep you and your estate out of a long drawn out court process.

That is where we come in. We help people just like you create a plan to protect you and your loved ones with the least amount of hassle, tax and expense.

Step 1: We gather and review your information and existing estate plan prior to our first meeting.

Step 2: We meet with you to identify the strengths and weaknesses of your loved ones and what you own.

Step 3: We take it from here and together design your individual Customized Protective Estate Plan™ to protect you and your loved ones and avoid taxes and probate costs.

Most people think it takes months of hard work to get their affairs in order. It doesn't.

Now you can leave the legacy you intend without the interference of the government or court system.

If you'd like us to help, just send an email to: **legalasst_sajatty@bellsouth.net** and we'll take it from there.

Steven Andrew Jackson
Attorney & Counsellor at Law
Asheville-Hendersonville, NC
www.StevenAndrewJackson.com
(828) 252-7300

About the Author

Steven Andrew Jackson, Attorney and Counsellor at Law, is the founder of The Customized Protective Estate Planning Solution™ and The Life Plan System™, that protect and provide for you and your family, avoid estate tax and probate costs and keeps your estate plan current with the law. Steve is a member of WealthCounsel, LLC. WealthCounsel, LLC is a three thousand member alliance of estate planning attorneys nationwide using cutting edge legal education and technology.

Steve has more than 30 years of legal experience and has been practicing in Asheville since 1982. His legal and life experience make him keenly aware of the need for personal and estate planning for everyone.

Steve regularly attends estate planning classes all over the country. He is a graduate of the Esperti Peterson Institute of Advanced Studies for Estate and Wealth Planning, a two year Post Doctorate Advanced Estate Planning Certification Program. Steve is a licensed attorney in the states of North Carolina and Georgia.

He is qualified as an Attorney and Counselor of the Supreme Court of the United States of America. He is also a member of the American Bar Association, North Carolina Bar Association, the Georgia State Bar, the Land of the Sky Estate Planning Council and the Midsouth Estate Planning Council. He is a former vice president of the Young Lawyers Section of the Buncombe County Bar Association. He attends The Strategic Coach™. He is a Living Legacy™ Certified Advisor and is the founder of

The North Carolina Estate Planning Institute, LLC.

Steve is an experienced educator. He regularly teaches professional continuing education courses to financial professionals, insurance professionals, certified public accountants and attorneys.

Steve is an experienced and gifted listener who hears his clients' goals and concerns. Together Steve and his clients plan to protect and provide for his clients and their loved ones, avoid estate tax and probate costs and keep their estate plans current with the law.

Steve and his family attend Covenant Community Church. He has coached little league baseball and youth basketball.

www.ingramcontent.com/pod-product-compliance
Lightning Source LLC
Chambersburg PA
CBHW071828170526
45167CB00003B/1469